Oasis Center Library
317 East Call Street
Tallahassee, Florida 32301

God Provides a Way of Escape

A Domestic Violence Response

Dr. Gwendola Williams

Order this book online at www.trafford.com
or email orders@trafford.com

Most Trafford titles are also available at major online book retailers.

© Copyright 2012 Dr. Gwendola Williams.

All rights reserved. No part of this publication may be reproduced, stored in a retrieval system, or transmitted, in any form or by any means, electronic, mechanical, photocopying, recording, or otherwise, without the written prior permission of the author.

Printed in the United States of America.

ISBN: 978-1-4269-8208-8 (sc)
ISBN: 978-1-4269-8209-5 (hc)
ISBN: 978-1-4669-2052-1 (e)

Library of Congress Control Number: 2012904441

Trafford rev. 03/13/2012

www.trafford.com

North America & international
toll-free: 1 888 232 4444 (USA & Canada)
phone: 250 383 6864 ♦ fax: 812 355 4082

Acknowledgments

I thank God for the gift of the Holy Spirit, for
equipping me and guiding me through the writing of this
book. A heartfelt appreciation to my family and friends
for their constant support,
encouragement and prayers.
My hope is that this book ministers to you
as it heals, empowers and comforts.

When you pass through the waters, I will be with you; your troubles will not overwhelm you. When you pass through the fire, you will not be burned; the hard trials that come will not hurt you.

Isaiah 43:2

for Pamela

Contents

Acknowledgments v

Chapter 1
Encouraging You to Heal 1

Chapter 2
The Reality of Domestic Violence 5

Chapter 3
Do Words Hurt?
The Verbally Abusive Relationship 19

Chapter 4
How Counseling Helps 23

Chapter 5
Counseling with the Scriptures 31

Chapter 6
Strength that Comes Through Prayer 41

Chapter 7
Comfort of the Holy Spirit 49

Chapter 8
Move Forward Through Forgiveness 55

Chapter 9
God Will Provide a Way of Escape 65

Chapter 10
God Says, "It Is Good" 73

Chapter 11
And at Midnight... 90

Prayer for the Journey 93

If you are facing difficult times, take some time to meditate on His word, these scriptures may be helpful...

...but God is faithful, who will not suffer you to be tempted above that ye are able; but will with the temptation also make a way of escape, that ye may be able to bear it...
I Corinthians 10:13

...hast not thou made an hedge about him, and about his house, and about all that he hath on every side?
Job 1:10

...but the angel of the Lord by night opened the prison doors, and brought them forth...
Acts 5:19

Bible verses are taken from the King James Version of the Soul Care Bible and the New Open Bible Study Edition

My prayer is that this book will prove beneficial to anyone who takes a glimpse through the pages, whether in whole or in part. Though it addresses victims of domestic violence, there is a word within these pages that can be a blessing to everyone.

Hear the cry of the victim... it is of vital importance for the church to strengthen their ministry to allow women and men to feel there is truly a way of escape.

1

Encouraging You to Heal

In the last thirty years, volumes of information have been produced about domestic violence. One important dimension of this time has been the new effort of the church to cope with the religious and spiritual aspects of these traumatic experiences.

This book serves as an instrument, introducing tools and principles to utilize nouthetic counseling as it concerns victims of domestic violence. Nouthetic counseling, as introduced by Jay Adams in *Competent to Counsel*, is motivated by love and concern, teaching, correcting, and using the principles and practices of the scripture to bring about a change in someone's life.

I pray it will empower victims and counselors alike through the journey to healing from domestic violence. I hope it will also acquaint the reader with the topic of nouthetic counseling, give tools in preparation for a more extensive study of domestic violence, and outline areas for further exploration. It may also create a dialogue in communities of faith and encourage victims to connect with those equipped to empower them through the word of God. I believe we will soon have a setting in which women and men consistently receive Godly counsel, and in doing so their violent predicament becomes nonexistent based on the strength they find in God. In the end, I hope the words you have read will provoke thought, discussion, action, and finally usher in healing.

The focus of much of the research I have done has been on victims of domestic violence and I felt I should link nouthetic counseling as a way to go deeper in this research. I have identified sources that devote some space to this area, and will serve as an excellent starting point. The message within brings to light some of the thought processes surrounding a victim of abuse and the place of God's word in their life, while offering alternatives within the church.

I firmly believe that a victim's exposure to this type of counseling will lead to an increase in escaping an abusive relationship and promote healing. I also believe that a woman or man in a violent situation might sometimes be shaped by the presence of spiritual and religious facets. This can be a blessing or a hindrance depending upon how it is viewed by the victim and how it is presented to them. I've learned that victims are able to cope in various ways, and the presence of faith and spirituality can be a tool used in overcoming their grim reality if applied correctly.

Consequences of religious misconceptions can be critical and an inability to effectively provide needed services to victims who are misunderstood and alienated could be detrimental. Without these competencies, society is likely to be a part of the problem, rather than a provider of solutions. My hope is that through these pages, I can introduce a refreshing way for the victim of domestic violence to look at their present and future, and create a yearning for those who strive to be competent counselors.

This topic is of vital importance because victims have traditionally been too afraid to breach the subject with pastors or churches (body of believers) that could be likewise, ill-equipped to deal with this issue. Victims need to know there is a way of escape and that it is through the word and nouthetic counseling can be a response to the violence individuals have encountered for years and may continue to encounter. This counseling is just the beginning of the work the church needs to ensure that victims feel safe and know that they can do all things through Christ; and this includes gaining victory over domestic violence.

Pastors and churches have a way to help victims by confronting in love and counseling based on what the word of God says. Within the scriptures, the God-breathed word is the answer to every question, and a solution to every problem, including domestic violence. Throughout these pages, I will address and encourage the counselors who are going to be presented with this situation, as well as the victims going through these trying times.

Children of God, let me encourage you today to seek healing. Let these words be the impetus that you use to further your quest for God and usher you down the road of becoming the survivor God has already ordained you to be. Allow these words to prick your heart as a counselor, so you can bear witness to the healing you are about to see.

Let me encourage you to seek healing from the wounds of shame, defeat, depression, embarrassment and worthlessness; physical, mental and emotional scars. Let me encourage you to seek healing with the help of our Father, who is able to do exceedingly and abundantly above all that we could ever ask or think. Get ready to lift up your banner of praise. I encourage you to heal!

2

The Reality of Domestic Violence

> Deliver me, O Lord, from evil men; preserve me from violent men. Keep me, O Lord, from the hands of the wicked;
> Preserve me from violent men,
> Who have purposed to make my steps stumble.
> Psalm 140:1, 4

Samantha was 25 years old. She met her boyfriend Michael, through a friend, he was 28. They dated for about 6 months and then decided to move in together. One month into this arrangement, Samantha saw another side of Michael. He became controlling and physically abusive; he would call her names and put her down, causing low self-esteem. Michael pushed Samantha and slapped her often when he became frustrated by something she said or did. He was very manipulative by blaming her for all the issues they had in their relationship. He would constantly blame her for every problem he had when he became overwhelmed by life's difficulties. Michael tried to control her by calling her cell phone all day and night and monitoring her whereabouts. He had severe mood swings, being pleasant one moment and enraged the next. Samantha was a friendly person, however this made Michael very suspicious, thinking that everyone she spoke with might take her away from him or come in between their relationship. Samantha tried to reassure him and did all she could to prevent his temper from flaring up. She walked around on egg shells every day and began to lose focus in school and at work. With her love and persistence, she thought he might be able to get through his troubles and change. Several months went by and they eventually married; Samantha thought that this would change him and help him with many of his insecurities and mood swings. Unfortunately, the verbal, emotional and physical abuse increased. They sought secular counseling, which only put a band-aid on the situation. As a last resort, they requested the help of a nouthetic counselor on staff at their local church...

The Dynamics of Domestic Violence

Domestic violence is the emotional, mental, physical and financial abuse of one person toward another. It is known by many names: domestic abuse, spousal abuse, intimate violence, dating violence and relational violence. It refers to a wide variety of behaviors used by men or women, to exert power and control over their intimate or former partner.

Domestic violence also seeks to establish power and control over another person through fear and intimidation. Those who perpetrate this behavior believe that they are entitled to control their partners. They believe the violence is acceptable and will produce some desired result. Therefore, domestic violence can be seen as a purposeful and instrumental behavior to the abuser.

Examples of this type of abuse usually focus on the physical aspect of pushing, hitting, pulling, punching, and grabbing. However, it also includes psychological abuse such as playing mind games and making the other person feel as though they are paranoid or crazy; and even sexual abuse such as forcing someone to have sexual contact without their consent. Keep in mind that there can be sexual abuse within any relationship including marriage. The other components some do not see as abuse are emotional abuse (name-calling and put-downs), economic and financial control (giving a partner an allowance or not allowing the partner to work), threats regarding children, intimidation, isolation (keeping the partner away from family and friends); and many other behaviors which, while all are not criminal acts, do reinforce control over the victim.

Although this book and much of the research focuses on women, men are also victims of domestic violence. Anyone can be a victim, it does not matter the class or race, economic status or religion, location or church affiliation.

Domestic violence is a widespread societal problem with consequences reaching far beyond the family. It is conduct that has devastating effects for the individual victims, their children, their families and their communities. In addition to these immediate effects, violence within the family becomes a way of life, and is the breeding ground for other social problems such as substance abuse, juvenile delinquency and other violent crimes. Understanding the complexities of this violence is the first step toward preventing primary and secondary victimization.

Some have the belief that abuse is a generational issue; those who perpetrate the violence are more likely to have witnessed and experienced abuse as children. For example, a young boy who has witnessed his father being abusive may grow up to be an abuser, and a woman who has been sexually abused as a child is more likely to be a victim of abuse or sexual violence as an adult. The list can go on and on... the effects are certainly far-reaching.

Some believe this to be a private matter, something that should be dealt with within the confines of the home or behind closed doors. The belief is that the consequences should come from within and not be the product of outside influences. Although legal remedies and systems of social support are now available to those in violent situations, it is difficult to imagine the isolation and helplessness felt for so long before these were available. We no longer have to hide behind closed doors; we can fling those doors open and escape.

****

She would move around from house to house until they became fed up with helping her because she would never leave her abuser... but she never had the strength... she was depressed all the time, about everything. If she could just love him more, he would stop hitting her. Her mother had stuck it out in her own violent relationship ever since she could remember...

****

How are those in the faith community responding to violence when they are confronted with it? The apostle Paul wrote that in his own life, he fought against violence. Instead of fists, guns, knives or hurtful words, he used weapons of righteousness; according to II Corinthians 6; leaning and depending on God for his strength.

God gives His people the weapons of righteousness to fight against evil and violence. These weapons may seem feeble to a spiritually untrained eye, but they are mighty in God. So "take up the whole armor of God" to stand firm and fight against evil and violence in the home and in the community. Fight to get your life back, your family back and your community back.

The faith community is not immune to the devastating effects of violence or the temptation to use it. Some have been victims, not only perpetrated by strangers, but by those they live with and love. Behind the closed doors of many homes, a secret violence lurks, leaving tragic scars on its victims and causing lifelong consequences. Unfortunately, victims have suffered in silence for years. . . they no longer have to. God cares very deeply for victims of violence. Throughout the Psalms, David cries out for deliverance from the hand of the oppressor. According to Romans 12, God has a tender heart toward those who have been victimized by cruelty and violence, and we can take comfort in knowing that a decisive judgment awaits those who oppress and hurt others. Hide in the word of God, allow the Lord to deliver you and embrace His word as your guide. We need to rally around the hurting and be the vessel God can use to bring victory.

What the Bible Says about Violence

God loves us and wants us to love Him, each other, and ourselves. God never intended anyone to be victimized, and it is important that we love and respect ourselves, holding ourselves in high regard. Men and women must love God and each other as the commandments require. Domestic violence is sin and violent interactions break the greatest commandments. Violence is incompatible with love and that is why it is important to embrace God's word to find out exactly what it says to us about God's love. Furthermore, we know the Holy Spirit neither produces nor condones abuse, for love and gentleness are Fruit of the Spirit according to Galatians. We are precious to Him.

We are valuable to God and His sacrifice for us proves that. No matter what we have been told, what experiences we have had, what mistakes we have made,

God loves us and wants us to be loved. No one has the authority to degrade and harm us. If we are in a relationship that threatens our mental and physical health, our soul and our temple, seek guidance and strength from the Spirit about how to bring life back into a peaceful place. We should consult with those who counsel with God as the center to assist in adopting a lifestyle that will bring us under His command to love ourselves.

I wholeheartedly support resources in the community that are not grounded in faith necessarily, such as safe shelters, medical and mental health facilities, social service agencies, and the like. These services, coupled with scripture-based counseling and support are great avenues in helping someone in need. It is a "whole-listic" approach that can be most helpful.

Women have lived in a world that has imposed its destructive actions of abuse, messages that bind or burden, inevitably producing guilt and shame. Most have internalized these destructive messages and now find themselves laboring in arenas that God never created them to labor in. God never intended us to be anyone's punching bag or emotional dumpster; nor did he intend us to be used sexually against our will for someone's gratification. According to Genesis, God has created us in His image and He proclaimed, "It is good". We are fearfully and wonderfully made, says the word of God. God smiled when He created us. He smiles when we praise Him, worship Him, call out to Him, cry to Him, and seek Him. Seek God, we no longer have to be a victim, He will deliver us.

Healthy and Unhealthy Relationships

Many people struggle with relationships in which there is distrust, doubt, disrespect, or hurt. Some do not know what a healthy relationship is and may not know how to properly handle conflict. Baggage from other relationships, toxic or unhealthy relationships, brought into a new relationship causes that current one to struggle. Communication is important in order to have successful and healthy relationships, peaceful and productive interactions.

A healthy relationship is one in which we feel secure. One that we are each other's friend, are each other's family, we blend our lives. We trust in and are confident in the fact that our partner has our best interest at heart. There are no secrets and we are not afraid to ask questions or share our feelings. If we let our partner know that we need them, they are there for us every step of the way. If we are hurt by them, we can share this and in turn, they consider our feelings, making the necessary adjustments to ensure the hurt doesn't continue. An apology goes a long way, and being able to do that, mean it, and work hard so that the same mistakes do not happen is essential in a healthy relationship. A healthy relationship is one that doesn't blame, produce hitting, yelling, grabbing, or denying that there are problems.

If we are hurt and make a request of our mate for reconciliation and they do not want to see our side of the concern, disregard our feelings, or make us seem as though we are "paranoid" or "not trusting", this is shifting the blame and not acknowledging the other's hurt. This is unhealthy. If we disagree with a decision that our partner makes and can only argue about it and not discuss it; or our partner picks an argument to make us feel bad or turns the issue around and begins to point out our faults, then this is unhealthy. Unhealthy relationships are also filled with berating questions or comments: "where are you going, who are you talking to, why didn't you call me back, why aren't you answering my calls, where were you today, I drove by and you weren't at work or at school". We cannot feel comfortable in our own world because of always feeling on edge and walking on egg shells.

We are always wondering if we are going to say the right thing or spend time second guessing ourselves as to whether we should say anything at all, and how it will be received. If we share with our partner how difficult something in our relationship is to deal with, whether is it their character or the decisions they are making, and they act as if it's not a big deal, this is unhealthy. If someone blames us for the bruises they put on us, or the anger they cannot control, then it's an unhealthy relationship. The first step is admitting that there are issues or concerns, and if someone is not willing to do that at the basic level, there will certainly be deeper problems in the future.

The abuser needs to feel in control, lacks adequate self-esteem and respect for themselves and their partner. They have a need to feel superior and have a sense of entitlement—this can be difficult to chip away at, yet can be done if they only first recognize there is a problem and allow God to change them.

It is so very important to look into our heart and determine what we will and will not compromise on. We must determine within ourselves what we will put up with and what we will not. What we will let go of and what means the most to us. We must also decide when enough is enough, and we are the only ones that can decide that.

Everyone should be blessed with a healthy relationship. That does not mean there will not be disagreements or disappointments or anger, but the follow-through is what the focus should be on, is it handled well or violently. God wants us to be in a healthy relationship ordained by Him.

Misuse of Scriptures Perpetuates Violence

At times, the scriptures are misused to justify and perpetuate domestic violence. Someone that wants to keep another in bondage may cite biblical passages and religious principles that can be explained in a way to suit his or her own needs. Sometimes these beliefs coupled with other factors interact to create an environment where abuse may occur and where it is less likely that women will effectively defend themselves and their children.

Please know that any religious teaching that is not good news for even the most vulnerable among us is a distortion of the gospel. We all should align ourselves with the word of God, so that we know which behaviors are acceptable, and which are not. Teachings that cause us to doubt our own intrinsic preciousness and equal worth, that cause us to mistrust our own ability to make good judgments, or that make us vulnerable to violence and abuse even within our most intimate relationships, are misrepresentations of God's purpose for us. The doctrine of God is powerful. However, distorted ideas about God are used to oppress and to sneak in control at such an abstract level that no one notices.

The challenge of a nouthetic counselor is to tear down misconceptions that are presented and support the teachings of love, respect, and obedience to God's word. The counselor has a duty to point out the scriptures that are frequently misquoted and direct victims to the correct verses through prayer. Meeting the victim where they are in their relationship with God is essential to empower and sustain them throughout their abusive situation. Counselors cannot force someone to be where *they* are in their walk with God; patience and understanding is important. Counselors also have a necessary duty to show God's love toward those who are victimized and encourage them to put away all false teachings and allow the Lord to manifest His presence in their life and direct a path toward a more fulfilling life. There should be a comfortable exchange between the one being counseled and the counselor so that the victim does not feel controlled and feels like a willing participant in the counseling and healing process. Knowing the word for yourself and getting it in your heart and your spirit, let's no one take that power away from you.

3

Do Words Hurt?
The Verbally Abusive Relationship

Death and life are in the power of the tongue: and they that love it shall eat the fruit thereof

Proverbs 18:21

Remember the old adage... "Sticks and stones may break my bones, but words will never hurt me". It can be a motivator to young children as a nursery rhyme or a song we sing to put up a barrier to our sensitive feelings. However, in all reality words can hurt, especially if they come from someone we love and care about, trust and respect.

****

Michael constantly walked around the apartment seeking a reason to "pick a fight" with his girlfriend,

Samantha. She was studying for an exam during her first year in graduate school and he decided to "out of the blue" berate her saying that she was unsophisticated and that she would "never amount to anything". She affirmed that she loved him and needed to study, however he continued to make degrading comments to her and say hurtful things. It was if he was one person one moment and another person the very next moment. She decided to put some space between them, as she had done on many occasions, and go to the library to study. Unfortunately, all this did was feed his fears and anger, and upon her return, he began to accuse her of cheating on him and continued to call her hurtful names. He yelled, "You think I'm stupid don't you? I know what you're up to". She tried to reason with him, but there was no reasoning with him. He stormed off in anger, drove away erratically and then called her repeatedly, harassing her over the phone throughout the night. The next day he apologized.

    This behavior went on for weeks; one day he was loving and caring and the next day he was yelling at her, calling her names, threatening her and lowering her self-esteem and feeling of self-worth. "No one will ever love you or want you the way I do". Those were some of the words he said on a regular basis to her. He wasn't always honest with her about his past or his current state in life, he kept many secrets and it seemed he lived many lives. He would even tell his friends terrible things about her to make her look bad in their eyes, so they wouldn't befriend her and would view her as the problem in the relationship. He frequently used profanity when addressing her, and although he never "hit her", his words would feel like a blow each time he spoke. Samantha became depressed and began to believe she deserved this mistreatment. She felt as though this was what love really was and she just had to endure it...

****

Verbal abuse should never be tolerated. It is used to tear us down and make the abuser feel superior. When the words are spoken, they cannot be taken back. Verbal abuse can sometimes be as difficult to overcome as physical abuse. Many times it starts out as verbal and escalates to physical. The goal is to make us feel bad about ourselves and cause us to internalize the terrible words that are being spoken to us. Verbal abuse can pick at our very core and cause us to doubt who we are, who we are in God. Sometimes the abuser will say "I never hit you", but in actuality the mere words cut like a knife with each one that is spoken. I've learned that those who are verbally abusive are selfish and self-absorbed. They feel the world revolves around them and if we do not give them the kind of attention they want, then they put us down to build themselves up. I once knew someone who was, for the most part, a very happy individual. It seemed the happier they were, the angrier their partner would get. Abusers justify their use of anger by blaming others, and tend to be very defensive, provoking and offensive. The key to overcoming this is knowing who we are in God, who He created us to be and who He says we are. If we receive this, then we do not have room to receive anything negative that anyone else says to or about us. We are awesome, we are amazing, and we are His workmanship. God said that He made us in His image and He made us to be loved, respected, nurtured and protected. When we embrace what God says about us, then we can love ourselves and not dwell in a place of self-doubt or discouragement when someone uses words to hurt us. His words are kind and worth embracing with our whole heart.

4

How Counseling Helps

Where no counsel is, the people fall: but in the multitude of counselors there is safety

Proverbs 11:14

Jay Adams, author of many writings on counseling, explains nouthetic counseling as counseling where Christ is the center, His word is the handbook and the Holy Spirit is the guide. The word *nouthesis* and *noutheteo* are the noun and verb forms in the New Testament from which the term nouthetic comes, and translated somewhat from the Greek, which means to admonish or warn. If Christ, His word and the Holy Spirit are not present then we cannot look at it necessarily as nouthetic counseling because these are important components in counseling with the scriptures.

In that, we turn to the scriptures to discover what directions Christ has given concerning the counseling of people with problems originating from internal or external factors.

The Counselor

The counselor should be someone who has accepted Jesus Christ as his or her personal Savior, and who is filled with the Holy Spirit. It should be someone who has studied the scriptures and is licensed in some capacity to counsel, whether it is through an earned degree or certification. It would also be helpful if the counselor has some kind of covering, such as a senior counselor, pastor or minister, to give guidance. The counselor should ask for wisdom and knowledge concerning the scriptures to counsel effectively and pray to discover God's will concerning the questions or problems put before them. The counselor should also ask for a revelation into the word to find out what it says about the situation with which they are faced.

In Romans 15:14, Paul sets forth some qualifications for counselors, "And I myself also am persuaded of you, my brethren, that ye also are full of goodness, filled with all knowledge, able also to admonish (or confront) one another." Paul says that goodness and knowledge are qualifications for excellent counselors and that nothing less makes one competent to counsel. The Holy Spirit uses counselors to right the wrongs by the application of God's word to human problems by using wisdom, or divine truth, for God's glory. The counselor must be willing to receive the outpouring from God and likewise, the counselee, must be willing to receive the outpouring from the counselor and from God.

The counselee, and for this purpose the victim of domestic violence, is someone who needs counsel or direction. They should be willing and able to receive what the scripture says relevant to their predicament and work toward a goal to effect change in their circumstances. If the victim has not accepted Christ as their personal Savior, this could be their first step towards healing. If this is not their choice at the time, they can still receive counseling... meeting them where they are... until they are ready.

While we may be flawed and imperfect, Paul reminds us of how important, competent and useful we can be to each other. Throughout the bible, it tells us that while our hope is in God, He has given us one another in our walk of faith. We should not live as isolated islands of faith, but lean on and learn from one another as we look to Christ for our strength.

Some things that should also be addressed by a counselor are the techniques that can be used by the abuser to discourage change in those they are oppressing. In addition to misusing scriptures, they may find allies within traditions or families to require us to remain in our abusive relationship. Fault may be attributed to us by pointing out, in some way, how we have contributed to our own abuse. We call this "blaming the victim", and this strategy is used often by abusers. We need only to believe those who have Christ as their center, and not someone living contrary to God's will.

As counselors enter the healing process of others, counselors should be aware that healing must continue to take place in their own life as well. Counselors must continue to read the word, pray and ask for guidance in their own life, while asking for the same in the life of the one they are helping. The counselor must constantly do a self-check to make sure that their life is being lived according to the will of God. This should be done daily.

Once healing begins to take place, important questions about the nature of healing must be asked. In the New Testament, Jesus not only casts out demons and restores people to family and community, but also restores physical health; the blind are made to see and the deaf are made to hear. What kind of healing can be offered to those who suffer from emotional, mental and physical harm? The same healing that happened in those days can happen today regardless of the need. Some ask the question of whether the scars left by the trauma can be taken away—can victims be restored to family and community? Yes! God's grace is sufficient. Jesus died on the cross and shed His blood and because of this we are covered. Covering by the blood of Jesus is healing for the body and soul. . . physical, mental and emotional. This was part of the plan years ago and how grateful we can be that it applies to us right now.

Sometimes it doesn't matter how hard we try and what we do or say, we may never be able to make some people happy, especially when their issues do not have anything to do with us. It is important to remember that we should try very hard not to own someone else's problems. It is for them to work out; they have to acknowledge there is a problem and seek help. Our goal should be healing for ourselves, taking one day. . . actually. . . one moment at a time.

Counseling Challenges

When counseling takes place, try to visualize two types of communication. The first type is horizontal communication between the victim and the counselor. The second type is vertical communication, with God through prayer, meditation, and reading His word. Both types of communication are essential in counseling for the victim and the counselor alike. Interestingly enough, if the vertical and horizontal lines of communication are drawn, it yields the cross, the one where Jesus died for us, showing His love so there could be a way of escape.

    A challenge that some victims and counselors face is confusion surrounding religious interpretations and the role the faith community plays in restoration; making this a dynamic issue. This is truly important because centers of faith are often an important refuge for victims of violence. Christian men and women may deny that abuse is happening, and may not go to outside sources for help. This is why it is so important to have Christians and scripture-based counselors equipped and prepared to assist those in need. Many times, religious misinterpretations distort God's word and contribute to the perpetuation of violence. The time has come for this to cease. Recognizing that this occurs and equipping the church to recognize it and counsel nouthetically is important in making these distortions an issue of the past. It may take months or even years to undo the damage this type of misinterpretation has done, but it is necessary so the next generation does not succumb to the plight experienced by their mothers and fathers.

Victims have tried to make sense of difficult experiences and seek support in times of crisis from various levels of faith communities, and it is not surprising that clergy are often the first ones sought for help by someone who is being abused. Sometimes, however, clergy may be perceived as ineffective in their efforts. If clergy are not always promoting staying in a situation that is abusive, then they can be vital in the healing process. No one should ever support a victim of violence enduring it for the sake of the family or to keep the marriage together. This advice may lead to a tragic outcome. All avenues should be explored, safety considered, the word of God used as a guide, and a complete understanding of the situation examined because this is crucial in doing the best for the person in crisis. Safety planning and scripture-based counseling should go hand-in-hand, when assisting someone in a violent situation. Addressing the long-term and short-term needs is also essential to the complete healing. A victim may not be able to receive the word of God if she doesn't have food to eat, or a place to stay or transportation, or clothes or diapers for her children. The complete healing is through

God; however I support utilizing community resources to assist with other immediate needs, remember it is a "whole-listic" approach.

When we are alone nursing our wounds, awake in bed with tears flowing, and wondering what to do next; we need a rock to run to, a hiding place, shelter from the storm. Counseling can be helpful if it strengthens and encourages and gives the tools to help us prosper. Knowing that God will comfort, the Holy Spirit will usher in a peaceful night's rest, and a remedy is found within the scriptures, we can be empowered as needs are met and healing is on its way.

5

Counseling with the Scriptures

All scripture is given by inspiration of God, and is profitable for doctrine, for reproof, for correction, for instruction in righteousness
II Timothy 3:16

Counseling with the scriptures is being able to use the word of God to apply to any problem, knowing the answer is within. Just as the counselor knows there is no unique problem that cannot be discussed within the context of scripture, it can also be said that there is a biblical solution to every problem. The scriptures allow victims to understand the problem, and allow the counselor to help them discover God's solution. The blessing is not contingent upon obedience to God's word without fail; however it helps to be aligned with His will. There is no need to be able to memorize or quote every passage of the bible, but it is helpful to become familiar enough to seek that passage when needed. He has made provision for the needs of His people.

Sufficiency of Scripture

Counseling is usually needed either because someone is personally experiencing and displaying sinful attitudes, desires or behaviors or personally suffering from the impact of associating with someone who displays the sinful patterns. The Holy Spirit must be allowed to renew the mind for someone to look at, interpret and understand life through the lens of the scriptures. It is clear, as in II Peter that the scriptures testify to its own adequacy and superiority. Consider what this passage declares about what scripture is and what it can do, and then consider the counseling implications of these assertions.

Believing in the inspiration, inerrancy and authority of the scriptures settles the issue of sufficiency, according to the writers of the New Testament. In a domestic violence relationship, where can someone turn? The scriptures address domestic violence along with other sins that can be overcome through God's word. Domestic violence is a sin, so let us continue to examine this a little closer.

Again, remember that II Timothy 3 tells us that scriptures are sufficient because they are holy (set apart from any other writing), able (to transform lives), inspired by God (God-breathed), useful (enhances life), and can equip. We have everything we need to understand people and their problems, and to help resolve them.

Misinterpretation of Scripture

According to Ephesians 5:22-24, "Wives submit yourselves unto your own husbands as unto the Lord. For the husband is the head of the wife even as Christ is the head of the church, and He is the Savior of the body. Therefore as the church is subject unto Christ, so let the wives be to her own husbands in every thing".

Some religious leaders and followers have used passages like the one above as validation for the perpetration and continuation of power, control and abuse. The problem with this interpretation is that it is selective and incomplete. Some passages are taken out of context and used for the sake of bondage, and to recognize this is crucial. Some neglect to complete the passage that continues with verse 25, "Husbands love your wives even as Christ also loved the church and gave Himself for it... so ought men to love their wives as their own bodies. He that loveth his wife loveth himself". These commandments are for both husband and wife likening their relationship to Christ and the church. If we follow this example, we can use it as a foundation for every relationship.

I Peter 3, tells us that husbands should honor their wives as unto the weaker vessel. A man is also God's vessel, but he is in many ways stronger than a woman. Therefore, she should be treated in such a way that is considerate. Authority should not be misused for the husband is to help, support and protect her, not to harm her.

Although many of these scriptures apply to those who are married, throughout there are instructions about how healthy relationships should exist between a man and a woman, whether dating relationships, engagements or friendships.

In Colossians 3:19, Paul tells the husband to love his wife, and not be bitter against them; the husband cannot live with his wife unless he loves her in the way Paul encourages. The love the husband is commanded to have for his wife is not primarily sexual or emotional; it is the love that God has for the world, and is the Fruit of the Spirit.

I Peter 3 also describes the subjection of the wife to the husband as a fundamental responsibility of the married woman. This does not mean the wife is by nature inferior to the husband, the way some have used this verse. If the husband follows the principles set forth in the word, then the wife honoring him in this way is acceptable. In marriage, two people become one through the joining of their intellects, their emotions, and their love. This does not give the husband permission to abuse his wife mentally, physically or emotionally. It becomes essential now that the church encourages respect and love among couples as well as help in lining their relationship up with the will of God.

As mentioned in earlier chapters, the clergy are often sought to help victims through violent situations. Some women, however have shared that those they sought out may have "made matters worse". Their clergy have asked them to "endure" and to stay in the relationship because their faith base does not condone divorce. Some have expressed the belief that if the wife submits to her husband, the wife can be assured the violence will stop. We need to make sure that the church is not failing these victims, giving improper counsel and giving advice in error to those who are hurting.

Victims should never be told to stay in a relationship of physical, emotional or verbal abuse; this may lead to traumatic ends, maybe even death. Victims need to be taken to the scriptures to find strength, and become sensitive to the Holy Spirit about what to do. The goal of the church is to love, and not stand in judgment of someone who is a victim. Neither women nor men should be turned away from the church, the church is where they need to seek refuge and be received with open arms. If advice given cannot be supported by scripture it should be set aside. Some centers of faith may be ill-equipped to counsel this special population and may do further damage. That is why it is imperative to equip competent counselors with an understanding of limitations.

According to C.H. Heggen, who wrote literature on abuse in homes and churches; there are four religious beliefs and implications that pertain to violence and can be related to domestic violence in many ways.

First, there are views that state God intends that men dominate and women submit. This is false. Genesis 5 highlights an integrative creation of male and female and affirms that both reflect the image of God. There is no dominant-submissive model that applies to what God had in mind for men and women.

Second, Heggen discusses views that a woman is morally inferior to a man and cannot trust her own judgment. This is also false. Some women trust men to determine right and wrong more than they trust themselves. Women who believed in this way of thinking had lower self-esteem than did women who believed in equality and partnership between women and men. Empowering women and raising self-esteem is an important facet for the counselor to explore.

Third, suffering is a Christian virtue and women have been designated to be suffering servants. This is not necessarily true. This does not mean that women must suffer at the hands of a man. This points to the relationship God has with women, for the struggles they may endure (childbirth for example), and the burdens they may have to help bear. In an atmosphere that glorifies suffering, women see suffering as their cross to bear, as a way of identifying with the sufferings of Christ. The nouthetic counselor's position is to encourage the victim to see that glorification of suffering may encourage the acceptance of victimization and may result in a minimization of the abuse. The counselor must also walk gently with the victim who is suffering and those who feel they deserve it, helping them find God's healing grace in the midst of their anguish.

Fourth, Heggen explores the concept that Christians must quickly forgive and be reconciled with those who sin against them. This is false. One of the most complicated issues for victims of domestic violence is forgiveness and reconciliation with their abuser. Although later, a chapter is devoted to the issue of forgiveness, this point is worth mentioning here. Those who are unable to forgive their abuser right away are sometimes shamed and condemned by their religious community. While the Christian community must continue to uphold the sacredness of the marital covenant, the church struggles to understand the permissive will of God in instances where the marriage covenant has already been broken by violence and abuse. God allows things to happen, even though it is sinful; however He may bring about a blessing later on. We may be pulled by a desire we have that may be against what He would want for us, but He doesn't give up on us. His perfect will however, is to do what He requires, and only then can we receive His blessings in full. Remember Romans 12:2, "And be not conformed to this world: but be ye transformed by the renewing of your mind, that ye may prove what is that good, and acceptable, and perfect, will of God".

There is certainly a personal empowerment for us that only comes through forgiveness. However, pushing for quick forgiveness not only trivializes our depth of pain, but may also rob the perpetrator of the opportunity to experience true repentance and redemption. There is no timeline for when there will be a change in us or the violence. As our walk with God strengthens, the goal of forgiveness is met. When we were created, God created a wonderful thing. We are fearfully and wonderfully made. God's word will empower us and sustain us, eventually helping us to escape a life of abuse.

****

The nouthetic counselor, Ms. Roberts, first prayed for Samantha and Michael and explained the secular laws against domestic violence. The counselor explained that although God loves them both, He hates the sin, which is domestic violence. The counselor also pointed out that Michael had been misquoting scriptures to justify his behavior towards Samantha. The counselor confronted him in love, pointing out where he had been in error and encouraged him to read the scriptures according to how God intended them to be read, understood and abided by. Michael was not very keen on the idea of having another woman tell him what he needed to do. He particularly didn't care for the fact that someone was telling him how to behave in his own relationship. Michael never thought what he did was wrong; he rarely apologized and blamed Samantha for their relationship issues. He felt he didn't need to change, she needed to change. It was important, however for him to realize that his behavior was hurting his partner and his relationship with God. It would probably take some time for Michael to come to this depth of enlightenment; however the counselor will continue to work with the couple.

****

6

Strength that Comes Through Prayer

Confess your faults one to another, and pray one for another, that ye may be healed. The effectual, fervent prayer of a righteous man availeth much

James 5:16

Prayer is essential in counseling; it is the way to communicate with God and eventually reveals change. Prayer should be initiated prior to counseling and at any point during; when the counselor or counselee need guidance. Most importantly, prayer should certainly come after and between sessions. Someone can pray with us and for us, but praying for ourselves gives strength and establishes reliance on something larger than we are. . . and if there is no one else to talk to, God is there. Prayer may be the natural outcome of a decision or commitment, it may be the fervent cry for forgiveness as the word convicts or brings confirmation, or it may be petitioning for the journey that is before us. Prayer feeds the spirit while making the word a reality in our heart. Prayer is fellowship with the Father, forming a personal relationship with a God who is more than enough. Prayer is a motivator, is effective and brings about results.

Praying the Scriptures

God listens to and hears the prayers of His children and the question may come up of how to pray and a good way to begin is to pray the scriptures in order to speak to a particular situation:

Father, I believe that no weapon formed against me shall prosper. I believe the wisdom of God's word dwells in me and because it does, I realize that I am without fear. In all my ways, I know and acknowledge you. I am strengthened and reinforced with power by the Holy Spirit which dwells in me. You are my strength and my refuge, and I confidently trust in you and in your word. Your word says that you will never leave me nor forsake me. I take comfort and I am encouraged in the fact that you are my helper and my way of escape. I will not fear or be terrified for what can man do to me? You will perfect *that which concerns me. Thank you for the word; in Jesus' name I pray. Amen.*

Praying the scriptures also means applying the words in the bible to a certain circumstance, maybe even speaking them aloud; memorize scriptures that the Holy Spirit can bring back to your remembrance during difficult times. We can hold on to those words of protection and peace while we are dealing with life's ups and downs.

Counselors should encourage victims to pray and make their requests known to God while also thanking Him for His blessings and provisions and rejoicing in His manifestation in their lives. God wants us to remind Him of what He says in His word, so we shouldn't be shy when we say to God, "you said in your word..."

Victims are not the only ones that can benefit from praying the scriptures. Counselors benefit from praying the scriptures as well. This helps them receive discernment and enables them to respond quickly to the situation before them, equips them during counseling and creates a total dependence upon God. Most importantly, it helps the counselor discover God's will concerning the victim and their circumstances. This allows everyone to acknowledge who God is, His nature and His sovereignty apart from themselves.

Effectual Prayer

James 5:16 proclaims in part, "the effectual, fervent prayer of a righteous man availeth much". Effectual prayer is prayer that is meaningful, real, useful, effective and powerful. It is also devoted, wholehearted and enthusiastic—imagine if everyone's prayers were effectual and fervent. Prayer is powerful when spoken and when heard. Prayer is integral for the counselor because prayer enables the counselor to receive direction from God. Prayers are equally important for the victim in promoting change. The Holy Spirit is essential in the counseling arena for both counselor and counselee; being sensitive to it assists in the success of the relationship. Many times counselors even work to intercede for people who do not yet have a relationship with God, standing in the spiritual gap for them asking God to work in the person's life. Prayer is such an important part of the whole process, it makes a difference.

We can believe that prayer connects us with God and His power is unleashed in our life when we pray. Praying is not just a way to comfort ourselves by saying pleasant, benign words. Neither is it a way to earn God's favor by trying to sound perfect. When we pray, we are making a direct connection with God. Prayer is powerful!

So powerful, in fact, that it can have a more significant impact than anything else we do for ourselves.

When we pray, we can ask God to fill us with His Holy Spirit, and once we have a relationship with Him, we can ask the Spirit to dwell within us. Relying on the Holy Spirit's power will dramatically help us hear and respond to God's voice as we pray. It will also help us express our deepest concerns to God even if we do not know how to put them into words. I have heard people pray, "Lord, please change him or her". But I have learned and have since encouraged people to pray "Lord, please change me". This can work wonders on how we forever view ourselves, our relationship and our life. We are no longer overwhelmed by what someone else is doing, if it's wrong or right, our focus is now on our self. The change we see within will strengthen us in ways we never thought possible.

Believe in God's promises within the scriptures and expect Him to move in a mighty way in your life. Have faith in His willingness and power to answer your prayers, and be persistent when you pray. Remember the power that was unleashed when people in the early church prayed; and look for God to respond to faithful prayers in powerful ways today.

Furthermore, do not try to follow any special formula when you pray. Just as God has created each person differently, He expects you to pray in ways that reflect the individual He has made. So, do not worry about a right or wrong way to pray, instead pray in the unique ways that best help usher you into God's presence. Some people sing their prayers, write them down, just say "please help me", whatever the Spirit within tells you to do. It is important to read the bible, think about what it says, apply it to your life, and speak portions of it in your prayers to affirm and claim God's promises. When facing a decision, ask God to show you the direction in which He wants you to go, and then commit to following Him.

Prayers shouldn't become merely laundry lists of requests. Praise God for who He is, confess your sins, and thank God for His work in your life, as well as asking Him for what you need and want. Know that God will always hear and answer our prayers in the way that is best. Wait patiently for Him to act in His timing and for our good.

****

The counselor spoke with Samantha privately and they both prayed about the difficult and confusing situation Samantha was in. Samantha began to weep and pray from her heart; naming the trials she was experiencing. She prayed about how she felt when her husband called her names; about not having control of her own paycheck; she asked that God give her the strength to not internalize the verbal assaults he flailed at her on a daily basis; she asked God to quickly heal her from the bruises and black eyes she frequently received at the hands of her husband; she begged that God heal her from depression and low self-esteem and then she thanked God for His presence and comforting her throughout her ordeal. . . and never leaving her. The counselor began to pray that the couple both hear from God to make their interactions valuable and peaceful, that they follow His word, and that God would give them scriptures to direct them and confirm decisions they would make regarding their relationship.

****

This is worth mentioning here. . . please know if a situation is too violent, couples should not be in counseling together. A lethality assessment is one way to make sure that all individuals are safe, and this could be as simple as asking questions about how safe the victim feels and if he or she is in fear. A few simple questions at the onset can save someone from further abuse in the future. Safety should be one of the primary concerns when advocating for someone in an abusive relationship. If their needs are met in this area, then counseling can begin; but if not, counseling must come after their safety and security.

7

Comfort of the Holy Spirit

"And I will pray the Father, and He shall give you another Comforter, that He may abide with you forever". But the Comforter, which is the Holy Ghost, whom the Father will send in my name, He shall teach you all things and bring all things to your remembrance, whatsoever I have said unto you".

John 14:16, 26

When Jesus spoke with His disciples before surrendering on the cross, He told them that He would not leave them comfortless. He told them He would leave them with a Comforter, which was the Holy Spirit. What a wonderful and precious gift!

Counseling is the work of the Holy Spirit and effective counseling should not be done apart from the Holy Spirit. It is the source of all genuine changes that involve the sanctification of the believer. Jay Adams, a leader in the literature of nouthetic counseling, has expressed that growth away from sin and toward righteousness is what sanctification is all about. In 2 Corinthians 3:18, Paul wrote of the growing change in which believers are transformed into the likeness of Christ, and concluded, that it all comes from the Lord who is the Spirit."

The Holy Spirit can fill us, and create an encounter with God in amazing ways. Therefore, during those times of the Holy Spirit's touching and refreshing us, giving us rest and direction, convicting us of sin, and giving us joy; we are experiencing the indwelling of the Spirit. The counselor and the victim must be sensitive to the Holy Spirit in order to receive direction to scriptures, in decision-making, and in relationship matters.

In the Book of Acts, there is a focus on the power of the Holy Spirit; what a wondrous thing, not an experience that can truly be captured with words. It focuses on the ability of God to use the Holy Spirit to accomplish many things, including releasing someone from the bondage of an abusive situation. An encounter with the Holy Spirit can come in our everyday lives and may be exhibited by laughter or tears, while praying or reading God's word. Have you ever just gotten "goose bumps" for no reason? Have a feeling of peace that you can't explain? God is trying to commune with you. He wants to comfort you, letting you know that you are not alone. He is with you every step of the way.

This is something to keep in mind. . . when the Lord fills us with His Spirit; He fills us with a purpose. Your test becomes your testimony, for you to reach back when the time comes and help others escape whatever situation they are in. Without your test, there can be no testimony of how good God really is and how He truly can deliver you out of the hand of your enemy.

Cooperation with the Spirit is a requirement of receiving the empowerment just described. This cooperation includes reading scripture, praying, meditating and hearing the word read and spoken. The Spirit empowers for the sake of growth through an abiding and indwelling presence, strengthens emotionally, and facilitates a change of heart and mind to overcome negative identities and affirm positive ones. We are who God says we are and He proclaimed that "it is good", we are children of the King and nothing less!

The work of the Lord to some degree, will remain a mystery, however what is certain is that the work of the Spirit is central to counseling for all involved to effect change. The Lord sent the Comforter so His children would find peace and feel secure in His presence. The Holy Spirit is God with us. . . He gave us this wonderful gift. The presence of the Spirit turns an ordinary situation into a divine encounter where true change can occur. Isn't that good news?!

Suffering and the Holy Spirit

Suffering covers a wide spectrum of human experiences and domestic violence is a part of these experiences. One woman's suffering is not another's suffering, but we may all share a common bond. Suffering is an experience of desperation—a longing for life as we once knew it or want it to be, yet understanding that life will never be the same afterwards, after the abuse. The disappointment and disillusionment of life in a violent situation poisons our thoughts, poisons our feelings, and threatens our ability to live an abundant life. Domestic violence victims are far too familiar with suffering, but that does not have to be their new worldview.

In suffering, we discover and understand that without God, there is no life and the thread that maintains a sense of balance between life and suffering is our faith. Faith becomes the hinge to the door of life, and the vein that carries life to the soul. In domestic violence, the suffering can be external or internal. Feelings of despair, depression, worthlessness, rage and shame may be covered up temporarily by the use of drugs and alcohol, not to mention other vices. It can manifest physically in headaches, stomach pains or high blood pressure, and can lead to such low self-esteem and hopelessness that it could end in victims harming themselves or others. Yet, our suffering can become a test of our profession of faith in God. It comes as a unique opportunity to glorify God. Our suffering is our testament that, according to Romans 8, "neither death, nor life, nor angels, nor principalities, nor powers, nor things present, nor things to come, nor height, nor depth, nor any other creature, shall be able to separate us from the love of God, which is in Christ Jesus our Lord".

Joy comes from knowing that God is truly our shepherd and suffers with us through our pain. God is full of mercy and compassion helping us when we are in need, feeding our hungry souls, and walking with us night and day. We can rest assured that even in our suffering, God is with us. Jehovah Shamah. The Holy Spirit is God with us and how comforting that can be for the one who feels alone.

We will soon take a moment to look at domestic violence as it relates to the healing of past hurts, remembered pain and unforgiveness, in which the Holy Spirit has a key role. Let's reflect and begin to put everything into perspective as we move through the rest of the book.

8

Move Forward Through Forgiveness

"For if ye forgive men their trespasses, your heavenly Father will also forgive you; but if ye forgive not men their trespasses, neither will your Father forgive your trespasses".

Matthew 6: 14-15

Emotions such as resentment, bitterness, hatred, hostility, anger and fear well up inside of someone who has been hurt by another. Unfortunately, these emotions can lead to unforgiveness. Forgiveness, in contrast, occurs when these emotions are changed to loving, compassionate, and altruistic emotions. This change occurs when the heart is transformed by having experienced the love and forgiveness of God. Interestingly, those who need to forgive must learn to have empathy for the person who hurt them, and have gratitude because they have experienced God's forgiveness themselves. A man who abuses a woman does not fully know God and has not experienced His amazing love. What a sad state to be in. Although it may be hard to show forgiveness for someone who has hurt you, it has to be done. It does not mean you are justifying the behavior, are weak or naïve, it just means that you want favor from the Lord by doing what He commanded.

Remember this; God's word does not say that we have to forget after we forgive. We may never forget, but our forgiveness can still be sincere. Who can forget the broken heart, the physical scars, the feelings of betrayal and loneliness? Sometimes it seems like every time we hear that song, or wear that favorite dress or shirt, or go to that restaurant, or go to work or possibly church; our mind takes us back to the horrible experiences we have had. Sometimes these thoughts can even come across our mind—of the one who hurt us—when we are praying, or reading our daily devotional, or meditating on a scripture… pray through it. We do not have to tolerate an offense when we forgive someone for offending. Please know that a person is not excused for their sin if they are forgiven; we forgive them because God commands it and because we hold them accountable and refuse to excuse them, and want to move forward into the blessings God has for us without the weight pulling us down.

In unforgiveness, we become a prisoner of past pain. The memory makes it hurt again and again and it seems like the thoughts will never leave us. Suppose we never forgive, suppose we feel the hurt each time we think of the people who did us wrong. Even still, suppose we have a compulsion to think of them constantly. We have become a prisoner of our past pain and we are locked into a torture chamber of our own making. Time should have left our pain behind, but we keep it alive to let it condemn us repeatedly. There is no need to seek revenge or plan to "get them back"; God will handle all of that for us. We can even ask the Lord to numb us to the feelings of hurt that we have had, in order to keep moving forward. Our own memory is a replay of our hurt—a place within our mind that plays reruns of the pain, and cannot be turned off. Only through the love of God can this pain be released, forgiveness is necessary.

Forgiveness is often thought of as a Christian duty. However, forgiveness can rarely be achieved when practiced only as a duty. The positive, loving emotions of forgiveness that replace the emotions of unforgiveness rarely flow from willful duty. Instead, it flows from a heart that is transformed by having experienced God's love and forgiveness. Escape the bondage of unforgiveness, repeated horrible memories, sleepless nights and constant past reflections; forgive with the help of God and continue on towards victory over your circumstances.

What Forgiveness Is, What Forgiveness is Not

Forgiveness lifts a heavy burden and means that we are no longer tied to the one who has hurt us. Do not worry, God will help us forgive. It is possible to heal and love again after being hurt and God wants us to forgive those who hurt us, in fact, He commands that we do. Why? Because if we do not, bitterness will poison us and we will not be able to receive all that God has for us. Here are some ideas that can help in the process:

Rely on God's power to forgive. Know that God will enable us to forgive anyone who has inflicted any wound on us, and have confidence in God's power to heal us. Realize that forgiveness will likely take time, but that it is always possible. Trust God.

Remember how God has forgiven us. Think about what Christ did for us on the cross, and recall the times God has answered our prayers. Thank God for His love for us, and ask Him to help us forgive through the power of His love.

Forgiveness is not an instant "pill" that makes the memory go away and it is certainly not a way to say that what was done to you was okay. We must pray about a particular hurtful incident, seeking to forgive, however know that this may not be immediate. This may not be easy. Remember that God has warned that our own prayers will be hindered if we do not forgive others, and that evil will gain access to our life. We cannot wait until we feel like forgiving because that may never happen. Instead, we can act out of obedience to God and he will grant us peace.

Also, remember to surrender any plans to take revenge because the Lord decides when and how to judge someone who has committed sin. Please understand that forgiving an abuser does not mean that we endorse the abuse. Forgiving the act does not change the fact that the act occurred, but it will enable us to break free of our pain and heal.

Do not make forgiveness contingent upon whether the offender responds positively to our effort because this may never happen. They may never take responsibility. They may never even say "I'm sorry". In addition, remember to always pray for the one who hurt you, that their eyes will be open to the sin that was committed, and that they will soon be able to repent and find the God you have found.

How do I Forgive?

Why is there so much importance put on forgiveness? Why is it that we are told to do this when we have been hurt, but no one tells us how to do it? There are many ways to start this process; we just have to determine the best way to reach this point with God's help.

Keep in mind that at times when we have done something wrong, that God has forgiven us. . . many times. Now it is our turn to allow God to see how His example and His grace have shown us how to show the same to someone else.

We can forgive from afar. Sometimes this method is best if there is an abusive situation going on, because we do not want to put ourselves in harm's way. We do not have to be face-to-face with someone to forgive, sometimes the more space that's between those involved, the better.

Helping someone experience forgiving emotions takes time and is not an easy task as a counselor. Changing the way someone thinks about forgiveness is a big step in the process. Forgiveness is letting go of the hurt and not dwelling on it, not desiring revenge, and releasing our self from the emotional attachment to this hurt. Changing the way someone feels about themselves and how someone feels about the person that harmed them is important. The enemy can get in our mind and have us thinking that we are the cause of our abuse and that trying to forgive the abuser is futile. That is very far from the truth. Positive thinking, forgiving and letting go, and moving forward in the way God wants us to, allowing God to change our thinking, will allow us to fully receive what God has for us. It will also help us to realize that we are good and that anything that is not good is not of God and not for us; God wants to give us His best. Forgiveness can be a long and sometimes difficult process; the pain will lessen eventually, and we will be able to close that chapter in our life, and start a bright, new one. Take one moment at a time.

Forgiveness brings Peace

Again, forgiveness lifts the burden, meaning that we are no longer tied to the person who harmed us. The abuser has already occupied too much of our time and our thoughts, so just think of forgiveness as "cleaning house". Put all of the painful thoughts, memories and betrayals into a trash bag, tie it up, take it out to the curb and leave it there. Now we walk away, walking back into a clean house; a peaceful mind and spirit. The only way to heal the pain that will not heal itself is to forgive the person who hurt us. Forgiving stops the reruns of pain.

****

"Samantha became numb to the feelings she had for her partner. She asked God for this gift of numbness. She didn't want to feel hurt anymore. This numbness created emotional space between them in order for healing to take place. It was a gift that gave her an opportunity to do some self-reflecting, increase her self-love and embrace a new way of looking at herself, her partner and their relationship."

****

Simply, forgiveness makes room for the Lord to bless us. If there is unforgiveness in our heart, He does not desire to dwell there. Do not miss a blessing meant for you by not being obedient to God's word and not forgiving. When you forgive, you set a prisoner free, and later you discover that the prisoner was you.

The Blessing of Forgiveness

Once forgiveness has taken place, there should be a change in the relationships that come afterwards, an increase in wisdom. That change, however does not mean that we must immediately forget the past. There is no such commandment in the scriptures. Forgiveness is not a shock treatment that instantly wipes out our memory of the past.

Forgiveness means no longer continuing to dwell on the sin that occurred. In counseling, the counselor could discover that although speaking of forgiveness the victim wishes to make the offender pay for what they have done to them. The victim thinks that if they could just make the offender hurt as much as they have hurt, then they would be content. Remember that we are still accountable to God for our sins and this includes revenge. These thoughts and feelings of revenge should be turned upward toward God, so we allow Him to deal with the abuser in His way. I have come to realize that God can deal with a person so much better than I ever could. It may take some time, but remember God is the judge. Also remember, there is no set timeline in place for forgiving someone, take one day at a time, sometimes, one moment at a time. With this knowledge and these blessings, our journey can now take a new turn.

****

The counselor mentioned the need for forgiveness to Samantha. Samantha challenged the counselor because she did not feel that she had the heart or the mind to forgive her husband for years of abuse. The counselor told Samantha that after she forgave, she must guard her heart, since it may take a while before she is able to find emotional peace. She advised Samantha to take more time for herself, apart from the relationship, making sure that it is only a temporary solution to find emotional peace, not an excuse to isolate herself from the world. The counselor also shared that sometimes reconciliation does not work because the abuser is not ready to take responsibility for the hurt he has caused. The counselor shared that peace is always possible. The victim is encouraged to pray for a heart of forgiveness until their next session.

****

9

God Will Provide a Way of Escape
Jehovah Jireh

"And Abraham called the name of the place, The Lord will provide; as it is said to this day, "In the Mount of the Lord it shall be provided."
Genesis 22:14

Faith, Hope and Expectation

When we approach God in need of help, we can expect our blessing, our miracle, and our breakthrough. Expect the Lord to move in a mighty way; a way we have never seen before, yet know is possible. Throughout this book, I have used the term "victim" only as a reference point; however I do not feel this term gives full credit to the survivor or the victor over domestic violence. The term "victim" can sometimes serve as a label or stigma so we must use it carefully. We can now view someone as a "victor" or "survivor". Labels only further stigmatize and bind; the Holy Spirit seeks to renew so there will no longer be a need for negative labels that define us. We can expect great things from God, and become an over-comer in His name.

Christians are filled with the Holy Spirit through faith, and interestingly there are many positions, practices and claims about the filling of the Holy Spirit. Accounts range from speaking in known or unknown tongues, a feeling, an emotional experience, an encounter with God, an inner voice, and a plethora of other experiences.

What one expects or has faith in functions as an absolutely critical variable in recognizing when the filling of the Holy Spirit has occurred. Although any or all persons with these experiences may be filled with the Spirit, expectations that do not fit a particular pattern may cause a person to miss a valid manifestation of the Spirit. Remember, it is an individual experience. Expect your miracle! Expect your breakthrough! Have faith that God is in control and that we can do all things through Christ! Do not force an experience, just allow the Spirit to move in His way and in His timing.

One of the first messages I delivered while attending bible college several years ago, entitled, "God Says I Am" illustrates the concepts in this chapter. When

Moses was told to bring the Israelites out of Egypt, he made excuses because he felt inadequate for the job God had called him to do. In the flesh, it was natural for Moses to feel inadequate and ill-equipped. Certainly, he was inadequate all by himself, but God was not asking Moses to work alone. God often calls us to tasks that seem too difficult, but He does not ask us to do them by ourselves. God offers us His resources, just as He did to Moses. We should not hide behind our inadequacies as Moses did, but look beyond ourselves to the great resources available. What He did for Moses then, He will do for us now. No matter what the abuser has told us about not being intelligent, sophisticated, beautiful or worthy; we are. Expect wonderful things from God. God provides everything we need, so we should place our hope and trust in Him because He is!

Psalm 4:8 states "I will both lie down in peace, and sleep; for you alone, O Lord, make me dwell in safety". The carnal person cannot comprehend this peace, however the spiritual person can. The Christian executes faith and seeks after God, something that cannot be done as a single entity. Faith stands tall and makes us stand tall, mounting higher than any storm or circumstance. Peace cannot be attained unless our troubles are turned upward toward God. Holding on to our troubles does not allow God an opportunity to work and give us peace. Our natural abilities are not enough to handle the spiritual warfare that goes on, we must have spiritual armor for that... Jesus Christ. We can have faith that the Lord has our best interest in mind, hope that never fails, encouragement in Him, and expectation that moves the hand of God. Take your bruises, your broken heart, your disparaged spirit, and emotional struggle all to God to be restored. Faith, hope and expectation are vital in the escape from abuse and important in manifesting complete healing.

Strength and Protection

God is our source of strength. In 1 Samuel, David was distressed for the people spoke of stoning him... but David strengthened himself in the Lord his God. During battle, David was experiencing a time of distress, however in this time of distress he realized that the real strength to overcome came from God. As the counselor assures the victim that she is an over comer in Christ, the victim realizes that strength is soon manifested within to help her persevere through her trial.

Keep in mind, that we are children of God and have complete access to Him, and are able to communicate with Him in whatever way we choose in order to build up inner strength. In due time, we will be able to tap into that strength when difficult times arise, and stand against the enemy.

God is also our protection. He knows the secrets held, the moments of embarrassment, the efforts made to cover physical scars, the terror, the shame and the disappointment. God is also aware of all of our needs; He sees the complete picture and provides what He considers as His very best for us. We are free to walk daily with God, free from the enemy, and He will protect us. He is a hedge of protection around His children before, during and after the abuse. His protection is based on His love for us and as our Shepherd, He watches over His flock.

God Provides

When we look back on the past, what do we see? Times of trial or times of deliverance? Do we dwell on the times that were hard or the times the Lord showed up? The Lord's mercy held us up then and will continue to hold us up now. Wherever we are in our journey God will meet us there giving us peace, protection and strength.

He is the first and the last, He is freedom and liberty, He is sufficient and He is God!

God speaks through circumstances; however our experiences alone cannot be our guide. God is able to help us through whatever crisis we are in because if we take a few steps in faith, He will carry us the rest of the way. We will never be in a situation that God cannot help us through; He has always and will continue to provide a way of escape.

Abraham was a man of destiny on a journey to a mountain of destiny and he could do so only as he trusted God. As Abraham climbed the mountain with his son, he learned God's sustaining power with every step. He was beginning to know the God who cares about the big picture as well as the small details. He wanted to be obedient to God as commanded and sacrifice his son; however God stepped in at the darkest hour and provided another way because of Abraham's commitment and obedience to Him. So we should remember that while we are climbing our mountain and each step tries our faith, that God sees every detail and will provide for us at just the right moment. Therefore, the next time we say, "The Lord will provide" and someone asks how we know, tell them "because He did". He provided strength, He provided protection and He provided a way of escape. What He did back then, He will do for us right now.

****

Toward the end of the fifth session, the counselor gave Samantha a homework assignment. She suggested Samantha keep a journal of prayers, meditations, problems and concerns. She told her to write down the date and time she began to journal, identify the issue she is having that day and pray over it. She asked her to find relevant scripture and write the scripture next to the problem. Samantha was also encouraged to memorize the scripture and pray the scripture whenever she encountered that problem.

A few weeks later Samantha revealed to the counselor that her faith in God had been strengthened since she had been doing her homework assignments. Her faith had also been increased because she was constantly reading her bible. She had begun to pray in expectation of God's movement in her life and the life of her husband. The counselor was pleased to see Samantha's growth; however Michael had been referred to another counselor because his negativity and lack of growth was impeding Samantha's progress.

They both continued counseling individually and would come together soon to have their progress assessed to see whether true change has occurred, if they are able to reconcile peacefully, and whether their relationship can be a Christ-centered one.

****

10

God Says, "It Is Good"

God sets the captives free! 2 Corinthians 3:17 tells us that the Lord is the Spirit who gives them life, and where He is there is liberty". Furthermore, to get free and to stay free is to be captive no more; we should meditate on the words of Jesus recorded in the Gospel of Mark. If we exercise our faith in God, the mountains in our lives will be moved; we must pray and ask and believe that we receive it! Please know, that we must believe (have faith) that our prayers will be answered and according to Mark's writings, forgiveness should also take place if our prayers are to be answered. This gives us power.

Sometimes the enemy looms as big as a mountain in our lives nevertheless; learn to speak to that mountain, in the name of Jesus. . . "Mountain Move!" "I must be set free!"

When we encounter the Holy Spirit, He is going to reveal the truth to us. That is when it is of vital importance for the counselor as well as the counselee to be sensitive to the Holy Spirit for direction. Each person must know the truth for himself or herself.

I am reminded of when the disciples were in a boat in a storm and Jesus was asleep below. The Truth was asleep below. Truth would later stand up and He would still the storm. Then the disciples knew the truth of their circumstances. Hallelujah! We cannot know the truth of our circumstances until we have heard from and experienced God. He is the Truth and is present and active if we are willing to allow him access into our lives. The word of God is a guide, a guide of faith and practice; and the Spirit uses the bible, prayer, counseling and circumstances to speak to us and show us the Father's will.

We may see our situation as overwhelming and utterly impossible to get out of. Certainly, the Israelites who had been wandering in the wilderness for forty years wondered if they would ever see the Promised Land. However, we must yearn to be free and be willing to take the steps necessary to become free. We must settle in our hearts that He alone is the bondage breaker, the way of escape.

Know this. . . our test becomes our testimony! What the enemy means for our harm, God turns it around for good; we can now become a tool of empowerment for others in bondage. God does not bring us to something and through something for us to keep it to ourselves when we experience liberty. Reach back and help that victim who is still in bondage to abuse and share God's word. We can show them God's love and help them to see there is a way of escape.

Strength made Perfect in Weakness

Our biggest weakness becomes God's biggest strength. We do not often view our weaknesses in that way, but we should. Paul prayed fervently for God to remove some affliction, "a thorn in the flesh". Refusing to remove it God said to Paul, "My grace is sufficient for you, for my strength is made perfect in weakness" (II Corinthians 12:9). That makes no sense for those who have not walked with God, yet we see throughout the bible how God is able to work despite the weaknesses of men and women, showing forth His power.

Let us look at David and compare his battle to that of a domestic violence situation. David who was small in stature was put in an interesting predicament when he faced Goliath, the giant; David (victim) vs. Goliath (abuser). David put his trust in God and was strengthened in Him as he defeated the enemy. In fact, the greatest demonstrations of God's power have come when men and women have felt their weakest. "Therefore most gladly I will rather boast in my infirmities, that the power of Christ may rest upon me... for when I am weak, then I am strong" (II Corinthians 12:9-10). Remember that the next time you feel defeated. Now I ask you, "Who or what is your Goliath?" Is it a boyfriend, a husband, a partner, an acquaintance, a friend?" Regardless of who it is, now is the time to escape your Goliath!

A Balm in Gilead

The Balm of Gilead is a substance known in the ancient world for its medicinal properties. It was exported from Gilead to Egypt and Phoenicia. Gilead is a location with its personal name meaning "raw" or "rugged". Physically, Gilead is a rugged country, and the Hebrew name Gil'ad may be translated "rugged". It was infamous especially for its flocks and herds, and for the Balm of Gilead, an aromatic and medicinal preparation drawn from the resin of a small balsam tree.

A nouthetic counselor explains it this way: Jesus was called a Balm in Gilead; He was the medicine in a rugged place, healing for the soul; he is the salve on the bruised place, and the Savior in your rugged condition. He is the way of escape from domestic violence and there to heal. Like a mother's kiss on a skinned knee, Jesus kisses us with His grace, His mercy and His love applying the balm to a situation of bondage; applying the balm to hurt feelings and scarred bodies. He is our Balm in Gilead; know that our body is a temple of the Holy Spirit, and no one has the right to defile or abuse it. Jesus can make the rugged places smooth, He is our Balm in Gilead, and He is our Way of Escape. Amen.

A Way of Escape

No one should tolerate abuse. When someone is constantly criticizing or controlling us, it is easy to develop low self-esteem and feel useless and worthless… especially if we internalize this. Do not receive it, cast it to the side and do not give it any value. Remember, we are made in God's image, and therefore are valuable and should always be respected. Remember, that when God made us, He said it is good. We cannot allow someone to turn their issues into our issues, making them something we are responsible for. Everyone is responsible for their own behavior and their own decisions. If someone is behaving badly and being manipulative, condescending, disrespectful, and abusive, it is because of something going on with them, they are not happy, want to be in control, or because of some other internal problem. We cannot allow anyone to use us as an emotional punching bag or dumping ground for their own unhappiness. We are more precious and greater than that, and above allowing this to be our reality.

Realize that God has created us to be a unique person with unique perspectives, and that we have a right to our own points of view. We should give ourselves permission to reflect on our present thoughts, feelings, and circumstances; and pray for God to give us confidence to share and express ourselves. If the abuse is violence of any nature, we should try to immediately remove ourselves from the situation and isolate ourselves from the person violating us. This is vital for our protection, however it can be difficult when it is someone we are in close proximity to or deeply attached to emotionally. Realize the extreme seriousness of abuse; it is considered a sin and a crime. Pray for the courage to escape from danger, we may be able to return later if the abuser seeks help and is able to relate to us in healthy ways. Also, realize that we cannot change the abuser, no matter how hard we try; only God can, if the person is willing.

We should take the time every day to seek God's will for how we should deal with a particular issue, especially relationships that may not be as healthy as they should be. It is good to spend time praying about all of our concerns and listening to God's direction through the scriptures and the Holy Spirit. Listen to God's voice rather than the voice of the person abusing you. We should be honest with ourselves about the extent to which abusive words and actions are damaging us. It is also profitable to embrace God's truth about who He says we are and know that God loves us and wants us to be happy and have the joy that we can get from a healthy relationship and knowing Him.

It is Good

When God created us, He proclaimed that "it is good". We can no longer allow anyone to tell us that we are not. We cannot internalize what someone is telling us when it is the opposite of what God declared. As Proverbs says, "death and life are in the power of the tongue", and when we realize this we understand that the words that are spoken can be positive or negative influences in our lives. When someone is constantly saying that we do not dress like they want us to, speak the way they feel we should, say the things they want us to say, act in a way they want us to act; they are depositing negativity into our life. Do not receive this. We are an amazing creation of our Heavenly Father, a gem in His eyes. Those who truly love and care about us should be filling our life with support, compliments, encouragement and everything positive that can help us be the best we can be. That, in turn, helps them be the best they can be.

I have talked to many people who have felt they deserved the abuse they received, and that something was wrong with them. I've tried to encourage them and allow them to see themselves as God sees them, and recognize that they are undeserving of any violence or abuse. Remember, God said "it is good. I've shared with some that they can pray every hour of every day, petitioning the Lord on behalf of their partner, attend church services every night, talk intelligently, dress well, and on and on. . . However, if their loved one has a problem with anger, low self-esteem, is abusive, controlling, or untrustworthy; and doesn't see there is a problem, change may not come. A victim of domestic violence may feel that if they love someone enough that they will change, I wish it were that simple. The abuser has to recognize that he needs help and ask God to change him, because nothing that we say or do will promote this change without the acknowledgment and participation of the abuser. Everyone has to take responsibility for their part in making their relationship successful.

Experiencing traumatic events in life may change both partners in the relationship. It doesn't have to change us for the worse; the experiences can change us in ways that will make us stronger and wiser. Just remember when all hope is lost, God is there. God uses our troubles to shape us into who He wants us to be. He uses our experiences to make us stronger and strengthen our faith in Him.

Being careful not to own someone else's problems is worth mentioning, because if you're someone with a kind heart and a nurturing spirit, this may happen. Everyone is responsible for their own actions and reactions.

Boundaries are so very necessary when we look at this concept of owning someone else's problems. When we own someone else's problems, we allow ourselves to become a victim of their circumstances, and this hinders the healing that we need. We are not responsible for someone else, they have to make their own decisions, and many times in abusive situations, these decisions are selfish in nature. We must decide what is best for our own well-being.

A young woman I know well explained it this way when she said that her partner was causing her to pay a price that she was not willing to pay. She was paying a debt she didn't owe. A relationship with him was costing her so much, especially her peace of mind.

I spoke to someone else recently who had been in a relationship for two years. She and her partner continuously argued and he constantly blamed her for his bad moods, the stress on his job, his family problems and anything else he decided to blame her for. The emotional and verbal abuse was sometimes more hurtful. He would say hurtful words, accuse her of infidelity, tell her that she did not care about him, call her at all hours of the day and night and just wear her down emotionally. He pushed her, left bruises on her, but always blamed her for it. He would keep her up all night questioning her or berating her and she would try to console him, calm him and try to reason with him. She would sometimes pull away emotionally because of the roller coaster he had her on, some days she thought she was going crazy. During these times of separation, he would pretend to be in some kind of crisis to get her attention and she did not realize this was a method of control. As mentioned earlier, power and control are the basis of the relationships that involve domestic violence.

He would say, "I really needed to talk to you and it was very important, and you didn't answer when I called", just to try to make her feel guilty and manipulate her. This was continuous and ongoing for 2 years, until he broke up with her indicating that he was "tired of the way she was acting, acting like she was better than everyone, and acting like she didn't care about him".

What a relief that was for her and what a load lifted, what a blessing in disguise. It hurt at the beginning because she had hoped all would be well, but then she realized that she was able to sleep through the night, pamper herself and attend church services. She no longer had headaches, she lost 10 pounds and began to pay attention to her own needs, and soon she started volunteering in the community. About six months after the breakup he came to her and apologized for how he had treated her. "I know that I put you through a lot and I'm sorry, you had to deal with so much and you didn't deserve me taking everything out on you". She still cared for him, but used wisdom and did not desire to get back into a relationship where these kinds of behaviors might happen again. She prayed for him and went to God, knowing in her heart that God would not want her in this relationship. He kept her in His loving arms during this trying relationship and she was thankful. She felt blessed because the outcome was such that she was able to walk away, because in retrospect it could have ended badly. She received months of counseling to create balance in her life, and is now looking forward to a healthy relationship ordained by God. He is ready to give you His best because He said "it is good".

A Little Note about Trust

Trust is the foundation of all positive, healthy relationships. Trust is the glue that holds people together through life's most difficult experiences. With this foundation, we can endure almost anything. Like a wrecking ball shattering a china dish, a relationship of trust can be shattered by physical, sexual, verbal, mental and emotional abuse. Proverbs 3:5-6 tells us to "trust in the Lord with all your heart, and lean not on your own understanding; in all your ways acknowledge Him and He shall direct your paths".

When trust is violated, it can be hard to trust again. When we trust someone and they violate this by becoming abusive, whether verbal or physical, it is difficult to see them in a positive light. It is important to know that not everyone is dishonest and abusive; there are many people who will treat us well, treat us with respect and value us as a person. I have mentioned to many men and women that relationships are there to enhance life not hinder progress in our life. I have told those I care about, that if they cannot deposit goodness into my life, I will not allow them to make withdrawals at my expense. If someone has been in a relationship for a long time, they may become accustomed to the ill treatment they are receiving and feel that it is normal or that they deserve it, or "that's just how life is"… "that's the cross I have to bear". Nonsense. It is indeed, *their* reality, but this is not what a relationship is supposed to be about. If someone has betrayed our trust, allow them to apologize and tread lightly when trusting again, however please allow them to show they are trustworthy again; they must earn our trust. They must earn it in the way that we need to see it, not the way they feel we should view it. Let the one who has offended know what they need to do to regain trust and if they are unwilling to do so, then maybe we should reconsider whether trust is the gift we give them again. It may take days, months or even years to regain trust, but if it means enough to the person who offended, they will do whatever it takes to ensure that everyone is on firm foundation again.

Sadly, sometimes however, the person who betrayed the trust does a few good deeds and brings a few gifts and they feel this should be sufficient; however it may not be what is needed. It is important to communicate what is needed to bring that trust back into the relationship and if it is not accomplished, then that person may not be worthy of our trust. The recipient of the offense is the one that can tell what needs to be done to regain it, not the other way around. If someone was abused when they were younger or always told that they were not worth anything, or felt they had to control all aspects of everyone's life, this is now planted in them, and therefore they live out their lives with this defeatist mentality, not expecting anything more than what they are receiving. Therefore, they pour into our life things that are not good, that are abusive, that are hurtful, and that are painful.

It takes a lot to repair trust when it has been damaged. Sometimes, all you really have is your word and if you cannot keep your word, your character comes into question. When we enter into relationships, it may take time to trust someone. This is what is called "trust being earned". We learn to trust others, by showing them that we are responsible and capable of such a high regard. We earn trust by being fervent and consistent in our life, not at one moment being abusive or dishonest, and the next moment not. We must treat others how we want to be treated. Do we want someone acting one way in public with us and behind closed doors, being physically and emotionally abusive? Some people have difficulty trusting others because they have had someone in their life that has not been honest and this leaves them feeling that everyone might be this way. It is up to us, to show each other God's love, treating others with respect and showing that we have their best interest in mind.

Again, once trust is broken, it may take weeks, months or even years to repair the damage. The key for the person who has offended is to turn away from this behavior and find another way to interact with the one they care about. The key for the one offended is to try to forgive and give the offender another chance if possible. It becomes more difficult to trust however, if the offender continues to be dishonest or hurtful, and this just draws out the process of healing and makes it more difficult to do so. Further discussion may have to take place if the abuser continues to offend and be dishonest, to discover the underlying issue that causes this repetitive behavior.

As I mentioned earlier, we are all responsible for our own behavior. No one has to abuse, disrespect, be dishonest or cause conflict; it is a choice, unless there is some underlying mental illness or other condition that causes the abuser to be unaware of what they are doing. Aside from that, the right choice for the offender would be to put themselves in the other person's shoes and see how they would feel if they were being harmed physically, mentally or emotionally. They certainly would not want someone to be dishonest with them, to push them, call them names, yell at them or talk down to them. So, why is it ok for them to do it to someone they say they care about? Accountability is the key here, but how many people have someone they associate with that could truly hold them accountable for their actions? We all need someone like that in our life, not someone who is always going to be on our side, but will be on the side of right and let us know when we may not be making the best decisions.

   I have heard from some that feel Christians shouldn't be going through these types of situations. I contend that as Christians, we are just as vulnerable, if not more so, to the attack of the enemy. What a great testimony, to be able to minister to someone and let them know what God has brought us through. We can use the experience of our trials and our deliverance to reach back and bring someone out of their situation in a way that we were brought out of ours. What the enemy meant for harm, God turned it all around and made it good. Even if we were not able to escape our abuse at the onset and have had to endure for months or maybe even years, we have escaped in some way, in a way that is allowing God to move in our lives for the better. We now can be a vessel the Lord can use to bring people to Him and allow us to minister in a way that helps us to heal, while helping that hurting man or woman to heal. Do not get discouraged. Keep seeking God. God has someone for us that will treat us the way we should be treated. . . God will provide.

11

And at Midnight...

Acts 16:25-26 gives us such revelation into the power of God and what this means for someone in a violent situation. "And at midnight, Paul and Silas prayed and sang praises unto God and the prisoners heard them. And suddenly there was a great earthquake, so that the foundations of the prison were shaken and immediately all the doors were opened, and everyone's chains were loosed".

In New Testament times, Christian believers were often delivered from grim circumstances through a miraculous display of God's power. Paul and Silas were beaten and imprisoned as troublemakers because of their preaching in Philippi; preaching of the good news, doing good, giving hope. While they prayed and sang during the night, the prison was shaken by an earthquake orchestrated by God and they were released to continue His work.

The enemy tries to get us off track and distracted from the work God has for us to do. We were chosen for greatness and the enemy knows this that is why we go through certain struggles. God's power to deliver is still available today for those who will exercise faith and seek His will in their lives. Despite their situation, Paul and Silas praised God, praying and singing as the other prisoners listened. No matter what our circumstances are, we must continue to praise God and show His love to others, we never know, someone may come to Christ because of our example.

The chains of abuse can be loosed; the chains of low self-esteem, anger, guilt, doubt, depression, self-defeat, and unforgiveness can be loosed. Your chains are broken! A prosperous life is now being released! God Bless You in Your Journey...

Prayer for the Journey

Father, you know that I don't know where to turn. I am coming to you as an empty vessel without hope, because I am in a situation I don't see a way out of. Please help me to see you and hear you. I want the indwelling of the Holy Spirit so that I can feel your comfort. I ask you to put your hand on my situation and be a hedge of protection around me so I might find a way to escape this violence. I feel depressed, worthless, afraid, and most of all alone. I want to feel your presence and know that you are with me. I ask that you work in the life of my abuser so he sees what he is doing is sin. Help me to forgive and help me to show love especially toward myself. Thank you for all the blessings you have given me already. I need to find my way and I know you are able to do exceedingly and abundantly above all that I can ask or think. Please help me to become truly whole. In your name, I pray, Amen.

God answers: "You have dwelt long enough on this mountain..."

God Provides a Way of Escape: A Domestic Violence Response focuses on how the cry of victims can be answered, and the victim can be made whole again. It is important to continue a discussion about how the church as a body of believers can nurture and emphasize counseling according to the word of God.

This book emphasizes the importance of counseling with the scriptures to help victims escape abuse in their lives. There is a need for them to find long-lasting solutions that starts deep within and can last a lifetime. It can have far-reaching effects, and touch every aspect of life, from generation to generation.

Dr. Gwendola Williams has had many years of experience in the field of victim services, which has enabled her to function in a capacity to help, encourage, instruct, facilitate, counsel and offer options to those whose lives have been touched by abuse.